Nelson ENGLISH

STUDENT BOOK 4

JOHN JACKMAN
WENDY WREN

Nelson

Contents

Units		Pages	Comprehension
1	How Mowgli joined the wolves	4–7	How Mowgli joined the wolves (fiction)
2	A Chinese story	8–11	A Chinese story (traditional story)
3	In the beginning	12–17	The Egyptian story of creation The Yoruba story of creation
4	Gale warning!	18–21	Beaufort Scale (non-fiction)
5	Wings	22–25	Wings (non-fiction, photographs)
	Check-up 1	26–27	
6	Newspapers	28–33	Newspapers (non-fiction, graph)
7	Fire beneath our feet	34–37	Fire beneath our feet (non-fiction)
8	The Ganges – a holy river	38–41	The Ganges – a holy river (non-fiction)
9	Caves and underground rivers	42–45	Caves and underground rivers (non-fiction, labelled diagram)
10	The days of the banyan tree	46–51	The days of the banyan tree (autobiography)
	Check-up 2	52–53	
11	Forests	54–59	Lord of the Rings (fiction) Learning about forests (diagram)
12	Bushfire	60–65	Bushfire (modern fiction)
13	Fascinating body facts	66–69	Fascinating facts (non-fiction)
14	Printing and writing	70–73	Printing and writing (non-fiction)
15	Earth	74–77	Earth (poem)
	Check-up 3	78–80	

Language		Writing
similes 'ure' pattern	verbs in the past tense	personal letter
possessive nouns		planning a story – characters finishing a story research – finding out about China
singular and plural nouns collective nouns		purpose/audience writing for young children research – thesaurus
better words		personal letter descriptive
word shapes punctuation	antonyms compound sentences	poem soft 'c' words
alliteration 'le', 'el' and 'al' endings	synonyms editing	newspaper reports – front page story
odd-one-out plurals of words ending in 'o'	synonyms	sentences – punctuation direct speech
adjectives made from countries 'ie' and 'ei' words		direct speech
superlatives root words	'ness' suffix	over-used words – 'nice', 'got'
prefix 'al' suffix 'ful'		time line personal/autobiographical letters
prefixes – 'dis', 'un', 'in', 'im'		classifying types of writing purpose and audience
describing a narrative picture 'fire' words		planning a story – endings descriptive
irregular adjective forms 'ible' and 'able' endings	auxiliary verbs	short story using 'age' words
present and past tense		interviews – note taking
gender words adverbs	syllables	science fiction planning a story – plot, characters, setting

UNIT 1
How Mowgli joined the wolves

It was seven o'clock of a very warm evening in the Seeonee hills when Father Wolf woke up from his day's rest, scratched himself, yawned, and spread out his paws one after the other to get rid of the sleepy feeling in their tips. Mother Wolf lay with her nose across her four tumbling, squealing cubs.

"Something is coming uphill," said Mother Wolf, twitching one ear.

The bushes rustled a little in the thicket and Father Wolf dropped with his haunches under him, ready for his leap.

"Man!" he snapped. "A man's cub. Look!"

Directly in front of him, holding on by a low branch, stood a naked brown baby who could just walk – as soft and as dimpled a little atom as ever came to a wolf's cave at night. He looked up into Father Wolf's face, and laughed.

"Is that a man's cub?" said Mother Wolf. "I have never seen one. Bring it here."

A wolf accustomed to moving his own cubs can, if necessary, mouth an egg without breaking it, and though Father Wolf's jaws closed right on the child's back, not a tooth even scratched the skin as he laid it down among the cubs.

"How little! How naked, and – how bold!" said Mother Wolf, softly. The baby was pushing his way between the cubs to get close to the warm hide. "Ahai! He is taking his meal with the others. And so this is a man's cub. Now, was there ever a wolf that could boast a man's cub among her children?"

"He is altogether without hair, and I could kill him with a touch of my foot," said Father Wolf. "But see, he looks up and is not afraid. Wilt thou keep him, Mother?"

"Keep him!" she gasped. "He came naked, by night, alone and very hungry; yet he was not afraid! Assuredly I will keep him. Lie still little frog. O thou Mowgli – for Mowgli the Frog I will call thee."

Adapted from *The Jungle Book* by Rudyard Kipling

COMPREHENSION SKILLS

A Copy these sentences. Fill in the missing words.
1 Mother Wolf had _____ wolf cubs.
2 The baby _____ when he first looked at Father Wolf.
3 Mother Wolf had _____ seen a man's cub before.
4 A wolf can pick up an _____ without breaking it.

B Write a sentence to answer each question.
1 Why did the baby push his way between the cubs?
2 Why does the writer describe the child as 'a little atom'?
3 Who was Mowgli named after?
4 Mother Wolf was very keen to keep Mowgli. Why?

LANGUAGE SKILLS

Similes

A **simile** describes something by comparing it to something similar. Similes often begin with **as** or **like**. We use them in our writing to create striking pictures with words.
Examples: I haven't had a good meal for days. I'm **as hungry as a wolf**.
It felt smooth to touch, just **like a baby's skin**.

A Complete each simile choosing the best word from the brackets. You might be able to use a word of your own which creates an even more vivid picture.
1 as steady as a _____ (rock, bus, jelly, book)
2 as straight as an _____ (ant, elephant, arrow, umbrella)
3 as fast as a _____ (sloth, donkey, bullet, bike)
4 as green as _____ (soot, grass, sand, cheese)
5 as slow as a _____ (deer, mouse, tortoise, hare)

B Make up your own similes to finish these sentences. Underline the simile.
1 He looked fierce, but he was really as gentle as _____.
2 Her eyes sparkled like _____.
3 He was small, but as strong as _____.
4 The stale bread was as hard as _____.
5 The clouds floated gently by like _____.

Verbs in the past tense

When writing about things which have happened in the past, we usually add **d** or **ed** to the verb.
Examples: live, live**d**   shout, shout**ed**
However, sometimes we need to change the middle vowel sound to make the past tense.
Examples: come, c**a**me   speak, sp**o**ke

A Write the past tense of each of these verbs.
Look up the verbs in a dictionary if you are not sure.

swim   say   run   steal   bite   sing   give   find   fall   throw

B Read the Mowgli story again. Write down all the verbs which are in the past tense.

C Write this passage, changing the verbs into the past tense.

The wolf jumps up as he hears the rustle. He wonders what it might be. He is amazed when he sees it is a tiny baby. It is standing nearby, holding a low branch.

'ure' pattern

A The **ure** pattern can be found at the end of many words. Copy this list of words. Try to find more yourself.

vulture	pressure	adventure	figure
torture	puncture	mixture	pleasure

vulture

B Copy these lists. Match the answers to the clues.
Each is an **ure** word. One is done for you.

Clues	**Answers**
1 A hole in a tyre	furniture
2 A large bird of prey	fracture
3 Exciting journey	creature
4 Chairs and tables	signature
5 Animal or bird	picture
6 A broken bone	vulture
7 Drawing	puncture
8 Name at the end of a letter	adventure

WRITING SKILLS
Letter writing

Balbir's parents have just told her that in the next school holidays they are all going to visit their grandparents who live in India. She writes to them to say she is looking forward to the visit.

> **address:** 4 Magadi Road, Kisumi, Kenya
> **today's date:** July 29th
>
> **people you are writing to:** Dear Bab and Beji,
>
> **start under 'Dear' / the main part of the letter:**
> Mum and Dad have just told me that we are coming to see you soon. I can't wait! It is so long since we were together. I miss you so much.
>
> When we visit you, can we go to see all the wild animals again? I would also like to ride on an elephant, and it would be good if we can see the peacocks.
>
> **an interesting last paragraph:**
> Please tell my cousins Harsit and Surinder that I am looking forward to playing with them.
>
> **a friendly ending:**
> With love from
> Balbir

Write a letter to a friend or relative, asking them if they would like to come to stay with you in the school holidays. Set it out like Balbir's letter. Your letter should have three sections.

- Ask them if they would like to come.
- Say how pleased you would be to see them, and talk about what you could do if they came.
- Say how much you hope they can come to visit you.

UNIT 2
A Chinese story

Once upon a time, long ago, there lived an old Chinese man who had a beautiful house and a beautiful garden. He was very, very rich but he was also very, very mean and never gave anything away.

The old Chinese man had a beautiful daughter called Koong-see who was in love with a poor young man called Chang. Her father sent Chang away because he would not let her marry anyone who was not as rich as he was. He wanted her to marry Ta-jin, one of his rich neighbours.

He told his servants to build a high wooden fence around his land so that no one could get in. He locked Koong-see in a willow-tree house and said that she would stay there until her marriage to Ta-jin. Now Ta-jin was very rich but he was also very fat and very old.

Koong-see was very sad. She sat in the willow-tree house hoping that Chang would come back for her. One day she saw a tiny boat coming towards her on the stream. She knew it was Chang's boat. Inside the boat was a message from Chang telling her to be brave and to get ready to escape with him.

Next day Ta-jin arrived. The old Chinese man had invited a lot of people to welcome Ta-jin so no one saw Chang slip in through the gates and hide in the trees until it was dark …

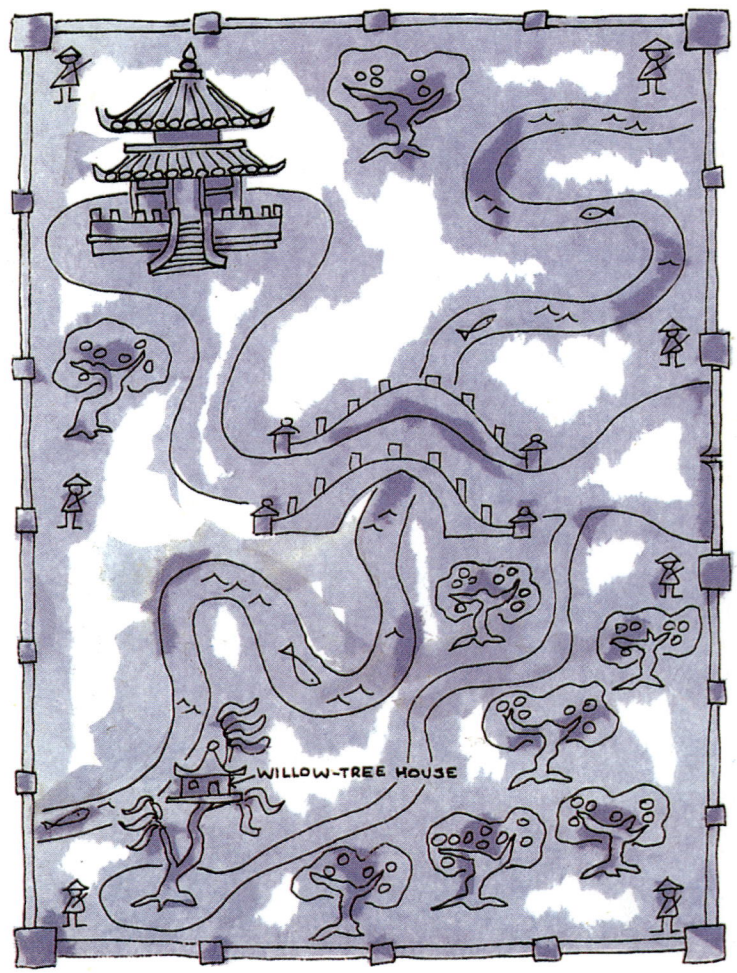

COMPREHENSION SKILLS

A Read these sentences.
Write in your book **true**, **false** or **can't tell** for each one.

1 The old Chinese man lived in a house without a garden.
2 He had a beautiful daughter.
3 Her name was Chu Yin.
4 She liked to read books.
5 Her father didn't want her to marry anyone.
6 The servants built a high, wire fence around the house and garden.
7 Koong-see loved Chang.
8 Koong-see and Chang were eventually married.

B Write a sentence to answer each question.

1 Why did the old Chinese man not want Koong-see to marry Chang?
2 What reasons did Koong-see have for not wishing to marry Ta-jin?

LANGUAGE SKILLS

Possessive nouns

To show that something belongs to someone or something we use an apostrophe (') and an **s**, like this: **'s**.
Example: **Chang's** boat
   (the boat belonging to Chang)
Chang's is called a **possessive noun**.

Write these in a shorter way. Use a possessve noun.
The first one is done for you.

1 The boat belonging to Chang. = Chang's boat.
2 The house belonging to the Chinese man.
3 The hat belonging to the old man.
4 The horse belonging to the soldier.
5 The dress the girl is wearing.
6 The shoes the boy is wearing.
7 The spear the warrior is using.
8 The plough the farmer is using.

UNIT 3
In the beginning

Nearly every culture has ancient stories about how the earth came into being. These stories were told to satisfy people's curiosity about the planet they lived on. The stories usually have a powerful god who was the creator.

Here are two versions of the creation of the earth. You may know another one.

The Egyptian story of creation

In the beginning, before there was any land of Egypt, all was darkness, and there was nothing but a great waste of water called Nu. The power of Nu was such that there rose out of the darkness a great shining egg, and this was Ra.

Now Ra was all powerful, and he could take many forms. His power and the secret of it lay in his hidden name; but if he spoke other names, that which he named came into being. 'I am Khepera at the dawn, and Ra at noon, and Tum in the evening,' he said. And the sun rose and passed across the sky, and set for the first time.

12

Then he named Shu, and the first winds blew; he named Refnut the spitter and the first rain fell. Next he named Geb, and the earth came into being; he named the goddess Nut, and she was the sky arched over the earth with her feet on one horizon and her hands on the other; he named Hapi, and the great river Nile flowed through Egypt and made it fruitful.

After this Ra named all things that are upon the earth, and they grew. Last of all he named mankind, and there were men and women in the land of Egypt.

Then Ra took on the shape of a man and became the first Pharoah, ruling over the whole country for thousands and thousands of years, and giving such harvests that for ever afterwards the Egyptians spoke of the good things 'which happened in the time of Ra'.

The Yoruba story of creation

The Yoruba people of Nigeria say that in the beginning the world was all marshy and watery, a waste place. Above it was the sky where Ol-Orun, the Supreme Being and Owner of the Sky, lived with other gods. The gods came down sometimes to play in the marshy waste, coming down spiders' webs which hung across great gaps like fairy bridges. But there were no men yet, for there was no solid ground. One day Ol-Orun called the chief of the gods, Orisha Nla (Great God) into his presence. He told him that he wanted to create firm ground and asked him to set about the task. Great God was given a snail shell in which there was some loose earth, a pigeon and a hen with five toes. He came down to the marsh and threw the earth from the snail shell into a small space. Then he put the pigeon and the hen on the earth, and they started to scratch and scatter it about. Before long they had covered much of the marsh and solid ground was formed.

After the task was completed, the Supreme Being sent a Chameleon to inspect the work. The Chameleon is noted for its slow careful walk and its big rolling eyes. After a first inspection, the Chameleon reported that the earth was wide but not dry enough. Later, he was sent again, and this time he said it was both wide and dry.

COMPREHENSION SKILLS

In many ways the Yoruba story of creation and the Egyptian story of creation are similar; in many ways they are different.

To decide how they are similar and how they are different answer the following questions:

1 Who was responsible for the creation in both stories? How were they different?
2 In the Yoruba story, who is greater, Ol-Orun or Orisha Nla?
3 How did the creators make things?
4 What was created in the Yoruba story?
5 Make a list of everything created in the Egyptian story and the order in which they were created.
6 Are there any similarities between the stories? Are there any differences?

LANGUAGE SKILLS

Singular and plural nouns

Remember, to make a noun plural we usually either:
- add **s** (river, river**s**)
- add **es**, if it ends in **ch**, **sh**, **s** or **x** (arch, arch**es**)
- change the **y** to **i** and add **es**, if it ends in a **consonant** and a **y** (cry, cr**ies**)

Write the plural form of each of these nouns.

1 night   2 sailor   3 peach   4 sky   5 dish
6 navy   7 fly   8 bush   9 daughter   10 box

Collective nouns

Match a **collective noun** from the box to each of these groups of creatures. The first one is done to help you. **A** = a litter of kittens.

> herd   litter   flock   pride
> school   gaggle   shoal

WRITING SKILLS

Presenting information

The two accounts of creation that you have read are presented as written stories which we call **continuous prose**.

There are many other ways of presenting these stories which will make them suitable for a different audience.

1 Imagine you are writing one of the creation stories as a book for a young child who is just learning to read.
   You will need to consider:

   - the types of words you use – you will have to use simple language
   - repetition of words
   - how you will divide up the story – what will go on each page
   - how many words on a page
   - pictures to help the child understand what is happening

2 Plan your book carefully:
   - How many pages will you need?
   - What title will you give your book?
   - Will each page have a picture?

When you have divided up the story and planned the book, use a thesaurus or dictionary to help you make the words simpler, and then go ahead and make your book.

Using a thesaurus

Using a **thesaurus** (or dictionary) can help you find simpler words for your story.

For 'hover' you could use 'fly'.

For 'countless' you could use 'lots'.

Look up these words in your thesaurus or dictionary and find simpler ones with the same meaning:

roam   explode   soar

UNIT 4
Gale warning!

When the air moves about we say that the wind is blowing. Sometimes the air moves slowly and we get a gentle breeze. Sometimes it moves very quickly and storms and hurricanes occur.

In 1805, a British Admiral called Sir Francis Beaufort worked out what happened when the air moved at different speeds. It is very important that people have accurate information about the strength of the wind. The Beaufort scale has been adapted for the effects of wind on the land and is still in use today.

Glossary
accurate means free from mistakes
adapt means to change something to use in another way

The Beaufort Scale

Force	Type of wind	What you can see	Speed
0	calm	smoke rises straight up	0 kph (less than 1 mph)
1	light air	smoke drifts	1–5 kph (1–3 mph)
2	light breeze	leaves rustle weather vane moves	6–11 kph (4–7 mph)
3	gentle breeze	twigs move a flag flaps	12–19 kph (8–12 mph)
4	moderate breeze	dust and paper blown down street, small branches move	20–29 kph (13–18 mph)
5	fresh breeze	small trees start to sway	30–39 kph (19–24 mph)
6	strong breeze	large branches move	40–49 kph (25–31 mph)
7	near gale	whole trees bend over	50–61 kph (32–38 mph)
8	gale	twigs break off	62–74 kph (39–46 mph)
9	strong gale	parts of roofs crash into the street	75–88 kph (47–54 mph)
10	storm	trees uprooted buildings badly damaged	89–102 kph (55–63 mph)
11	violent storm	general destruction	103–117 kph (64–72 mph)
12	hurricane	coasts flooded devastation	over 117 kph (73 mph or more)

Glossary *kph* means kilometres per hour   *mph* means miles per hour

COMPREHENSION SKILLS

Look at the chart and answer the questions.
1. What can you see when there is a strong breeze?
2. What speed is the wind when there is a hurricane blowing?
3. What is the type of wind when you can see twigs breaking off?
4. What is the force of the wind when it is travelling at 30-39 kph?

UNIT 5
Wings

Birds have many shapes and sizes of wings. The type of wing depends on the way the bird lives and needs to be able to fly. People have tried to copy the birds. You can tell by looking at the wings of aeroplanes what sort of flying they are designed to do.

Long wings are best for gliding. Most sea gulls have long, slim wings and can glide across the seas and oceans for hundreds of kilometres. This albatross glides so well it can even sleep while flying.

Short wings let a bird twist and turn sharply. Birds like this kingfisher have short wings as they need to twist and turn among the branches of trees, and swoop and dive for fish in rivers.

Wide wings are best for soaring. This eagle, like many other birds of prey, can soar high in the sky as it looks for food.

COMPREHENSION SKILLS

A Copy these sentences. Fill in the missing words.

1 _____ wings are best for gliding.

2 Birds that twist and turn quickly usually have _____ wings.

3 An eagle has _____ wings.

4 Wide wings are best for _____ .

B Write a sentence to answer each question.

1 What are the wings of a sea gull like?

2 Which bird can sleep while it flies?

3 Why do birds of prey need to soar?

4 Look at the photograph above.
   What sort of flying does this plane do?

LANGUAGE SKILLS

Word shapes

TALL SHORT

Write these words in such a way that their shapes give a clue to their meanings. If you have time, make a few more.

| long | narrow | twist | sleep | soar |

Antonyms

Write the antonym for each of these words. Remember, antonyms are words with opposite meanings.

| high | in | short | straight | up | top | wide | below |
| cover | fair | lucky | honest | correct | efficient | | |

23

Punctuation marks

Write these sentences correctly.

1 Do you enjoy bird-watching
2 The huge albatross has long sleek graceful wings
3 This bird has a broken wing said the old lady
4 In jamaica said wesley dreamily the birds have such wonderful colours

Compound sentences

Conjunctions stick sentences together.

Simple sentences can be joined together by **conjunctions** to make a **compound sentence**. In the sentence below **and** is the conjunction.
Example: The kingfisher has short wings. Its feathers are brightly coloured.
The kingfisher has short wings **and** its feathers are brightly coloured.

A Join these sentences together with the conjunctions **and** or **but**.

1 Humans can fly. They need machines to help them.
2 The bird flies fast. It catches the moth.
3 The eagle circles over a mouse. The little animal escapes.
4 Gliders fly slowly. Jet planes fly quickly.
5 I like bird-watching. I enjoy drawing birds.

B Write these sentences, choosing **until, so, because** or **but** as the conjunction to complete them.

1 I hid behind the hedge _____ I could see the birds.
2 The keeper wears a thick glove _____ the eagle has sharp claws.
3 The gull glided along the cliff _____ it reached its nesting place.
4 Short wings are good for twisting and turning _____ long wings are better for gliding.

WRITING SKILLS

Poems using soft 'c' words

When the letter **c** sounds like a letter **s** we say it is 'soft'.
Example: face

A Read this limerick. Limericks have five lines, with the first, second and fifth lines rhyming.

There was an old man, Vince Price,
Who loved his little pet mice,
Until by chance
He saw with a glance
They were eating his curry and rice.

B Make up a poem of your own. It could be a limerick.
You may find some of the rhyming words in the box useful.

nice	palace	mince	chance	lice	place
since	dance	rice	face	glance	ice	race

25

Check-up 1

VOCABULARY

A Complete each simile using the best word from the brackets.
  1 as strong as an _____ (ox, ant, octopus)
  2 as quiet as a _____ (hyena, mouse, bee)
  3 as small as an _____ (elephant, ant-eater, ant)

B Complete each simile using a word of your own.
  1 The elephant's skin was like _____ to touch.
  2 The wind roared like a _____ .
  3 After the long run my legs felt like _____ .

C Think of three ways to write 'it was raining' in a more interesting and descriptive way.

D Write an antonym for each of these words.

| happy | quick | heavy | under |
| on | hot | honest | correct |

PUNCTUATION

A Write a short letter to a friend telling them about your visit to the zoo. Say what you liked, and what you didn't like.
Set out your letter carefully. Remember to start and finish it properly.

B Look at these sentences. The punctuation marks and capital letters have been missed out.
Write the sentences correctly.
  1 can i keep a pet lion cub asked aziz
  2 no you most certainly cannot retorted his mother
  3 why not said aziz they are so soft and cuddly
  4 yes but they grow up big and not so cuddly laughed his father

GRAMMAR

A Write these verbs in the past tense.

> walk   live   say   sing   give   throw   swim   fall

B Write these phrases in a shorter way using possessive nouns.
1. the paw of the lion
2. the tail belonging to the dog
3. the horse belonging to the rider
4. the furry coat of the animal
5. the sharp teeth of the leopard

C Use conjunctions to join these pairs of sentences.
1. I hid behind the bush. The elephant could sense I was there.
2. I was scared. I decided to run.
3. It was a foolish thing to do. I was lucky to escape unhurt.

SPELLING

A Finish these **ure** pattern words.
1. f_____   tables and chairs
2. v_____   large meat-eating bird
3. cr_____ s   birds and animals

B Add the missing letter **c** or **s** to these words.

ni_e   ri_e   plea_e   i_e

ra_e   wa_p   dan_e   fen_e

UNIT 6
Newspapers

Newspapers can be used to tell us many things – not just the news!

This graph shows us which letters we use the most.
Make a graph like this yourself, and see if you get a similar answer.
- First take a local or national, English-speaking newspaper. Choose 100 words from anywhere in the newspaper.
- Count how often each letter occurs in the 100 words.
- Draw a bar graph to show your results.

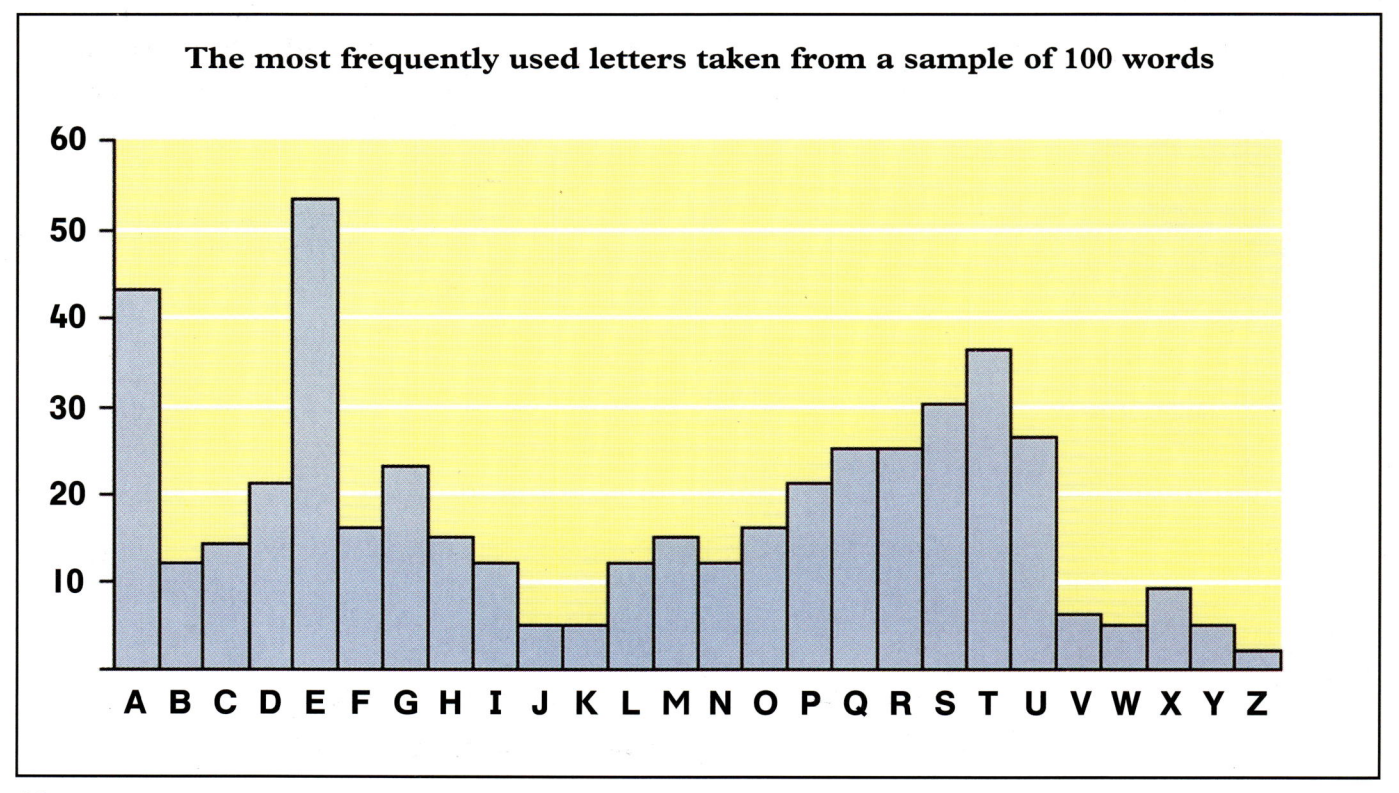

The most frequently used letters taken from a sample of 100 words

Which newspaper uses longer words? Which newspaper is easier to read?

- Find copies of two or three different newspapers or magazines.
- Count about 100 words in a story in each newspaper. Work out how many words have one letter, two letters, three letters and so on.
- For each newspaper make a simple graph to show how many letters the words have. In the first column record how many one-letter words there are, in the next column how many two-letter words there are, and so on.

COMPREHENSION SKILLS

A Copy these sentences. Fill in the missing words or letters.

1 The most frequently used letter in the newspapers is _____.

2 The most common consonant is _____.

3 I found that _____ has the longest words.

4 My favourite newspaper or magazine is _____.

B Write sentences to answer each question.

1 How many different stories are there on the front page of each of the newspapers you have looked at?

2 Which story did you find most interesting?

3 Which newspaper did you most enjoy reading?

4 Why are most newspaper headlines very short?

LANGUAGE SKILLS

Alliteration

Round the **r**ugged **r**ock, the **r**agged **r**ascal **r**an.

Repeating the same sound at the beginning of two or more words is called **alliteration**. You will often see alliteration used for headlines in newspapers.

Heavy hailstorm hits Harare

Farmer's fields flooded in Farndon!

Record rainfall in Rangoon

Make up headlines for these stories using alliteration.

1 Unusual weather conditions in your area.
2 Tennis championship success for your school.

Synonyms

Your dictionary and thesaurus will help you.

A Journalists need to use words which are easy for people to read and understand. Read these sentences. Find other words which have a similar meaning to the underlined words.

1 They thought the house had been vacant.
2 There was concern that someone had broken in.
3 Having completed the search they had found nothing.
4 The adjacent house was also damaged.
5 The police said they would observe the boys from a distance.
6 The officer apprehended the suspect.
7 He said he went into the shop to purchase some sweets.
8 She couldn't comprehend why anyone should steal her money.

'le', 'el' and 'al' endings

A There are hundreds of words that end in **le**, **el** or **al**.

1 Look through your reading book for a few minutes and make a list of words ending in **le**, el or **al**.

2 Count how many words you have collected with each ending.

3 Which ending is the most common?

B Look at the words in the box.

towel	capital	tunnel	equal	animal
signal	eagle	people	kettle	little	vessel
circle	twinkle	festival	jewel

1 Choose four **le** words, four **el** words and four **al** words.

2 Learn these words and ask a friend to test you.

Look
Cover
Remember
Write
Check

C Here are 20 words which need an ending. Add **le**, **el** or **al** to each one to make a different word. Your dictionary will help you.

tab__	kett__	tunn__	barr__	whist__
actu__	cam__	troub__	hand__	met__
unc__	cast__	usu__	arriv__	ang__	ang__
tick__	bib__	fe__	triang__

Editing

Pretend you work for your local newspaper. Someone has seen a terrible fire and written to the newspaper, but he cannot write very well. Your editor wants you to rewrite the piece, correcting the punctuation, spelling and other mistakes.

Wot a shok i got. Ther i woz on me way home wen i sor this grate flash. Help Help me i herd the old laddy crie from the winder so i dashed akross and got the ladder whot woz by the fense. stay ther i screemed. please bee quik she called. i just got her out as the fire ingine got ther. that was a cloze thing sed the firefighter weel done we wil macke yuo a firefighter eny day sed the fire cheif

31

UNIT 7
Fire beneath our feet

Deep in the centre of the Earth the rocks are not cold and hard, but extremely hot, which makes them molten, like thick syrup. This hot rock is called 'magma'.

Sometimes this hot magma forces its way up cracks to the surface of the Earth. Great clouds of ash and gases burst out at the same time. The magma is called 'lava' once it has escaped.

When the magma reaches the surface, the great fiery mass of lava and ash makes a 'volcano'. As the hot rocks cool they become hard. After a while, some of the hard lava blocks the opening of the volcano, like a cork in a bottle. This is called a 'plug'. Soon the volcano becomes quiet. However, old, quiet volcanoes sometimes unexpectedly erupt into life again – with devastating consequences for those who live nearby!

One of the largest eruptions for many years was Mount Pinatubo in the Philippines, which erupted on 15th June 1991. The ash and dust thrown into the air made the world's weather cooler for several years.

COMPREHENSION SKILLS

A Copy these sentences. Fill in the missing words.

1 Deep in the Earth the rocks are very _____ .

2 This hot rock is called _____ .

3 _____ are formed when the lava and ash escape at the surface.

4 Mount Pinatubo erupted on _____ .

B Write a sentence to answer each question.

1 Why are the rocks in the centre of the Earth 'like thick syrup'?

2 When does 'magma' become known as 'lava'?

3 Find a simile in the passage.

4 What effect can volcanoes have on the weather?

LANGUAGE SKILLS

Odd-one-out

Find the odd-one-out in these groups of words.
Give your reason for each answer.

1 rock, lava, sand, stone, sugar

2 volcano, village, mountain, hill, valley

3 plug, ash, magma, gas, grass

4 magma, water, milk, wood, syrup

Synonyms

Which word in brackets is the synonym of these words?
Remember, synonyms have similar meanings.

1 molten (melted, solid, thick, heavy)
2 centre (circle, middle, edge, corner)
3 thrown (propelled, dropped, ball, through)
4 extremely (very, usually, tiny, slow)

Plurals
Words ending in 'o'

> We add **es** to most words ending in **o** to make them plural.
> *Example:* one volcano   two volcano**es**
> However, for musical words ending in **o**, and for words ending in **oo**, we just add **s**.
> *Examples:* one piano, two piano**s**   one cuckoo, two cuckoo**s**
> Be careful, remember these exceptions to the rules:
> **photos   hippos   radios   rhinos**

Write the plural of each of these words. Look carefully at the rules. Use your dictionary to help you.

> hero   cockatoo   bamboo   echo   alto   tomato
> motto   soprano   photo   cello   potato

WRITING SKILLS

Sentences

A This is one sentence. All the spaces, capital letters, apostrophes and full stops have been taken out. Write it out properly.

averyfamousvolcanoisvesuviusinitalywhichkilledmanypeopleinthetownofpompeii

B Write these sentences. Put in the capital letters, commas, full stops, question marks and exclamation marks.

1 there are volcanoes in the philippines
2 have you seen mount pinatubo
3 ouch that was hot
4 the hot swirling molten lava engulfed the buildings

Direct speech

Write these sentences and add the inverted commas (speech marks). Remember, only the words actually spoken should be inside the inverted commas.

1 It erupted last year, warned our guide.
= "It erupted last year," warned our guide.
2 You may find it a steep climb up, he said. However, it's an easy walk down.
3 If you look carefully, he shouted, you will be able to see the lava bubbling.
4 Tom was scared. I don't like being so close to a volcano, he said.

UNIT 8
The Ganges – a holy river

The Ganges is India's most famous river. It is about 2500 kilometres long and two hundred million people live in its valley.

Hindu people believe that the Ganges is a holy river, so every year millions of them travel along it. Many go by bus or train, but some very fit people walk all the way, which can take six years.

Many holy men live in the hills near the source of the river. They claim to be able to tell the future, heal the sick and get rid of bad luck. Some holy men do not eat for many weeks and wear only a thin cotton cloth in the bitter snows of Winter.

Hindus believe that the waters of the Ganges have special powers to heal sick people, and that their sins are washed away if they bathe in it.

The largest city on the banks of the Ganges is Calcutta. It is one of the most crowded cities in the world. The most famous holy city along the Ganges is Varanasi, which has many beautiful temples and religious museums.

The Ganges is not only important as a holy river. Farmers use it to water their crops, and the river has many fish which people can catch to eat or sell.

COMPREHENSION SKILLS

A Copy these sentences. Fill in the missing words.

1 The _____ is the most famous river in India.

2 It is a holy river for the _____ people.

3 It can take _____ years to walk the length of the River Ganges.

4 The largest city on the Ganges is _____.

B Write a sentence to answer each question.

1 How many people live in the Ganges Valley?

2 Why do people want to journey along the Ganges?

3 Why is Varanasi famous?

4 The Ganges is important to farmers, but why might they sometimes regret being in its valley?

C Use an atlas to find the countries or continents where these rivers are to be found.

| Thames | Mississippi | Congo | Amazon | Nile | Danube |
| Volga | Seine | Murray | Rhine | Yangtze |

LANGUAGE SKILLS

Adjectives made from countries

Country names are proper nouns, so always start them with a capital letter.

Adjectives ('describing' words) can be made from the names of countries.
- To make adjectives from most countries ending in **a**, we add an **n**. *Example:* India = India**n**.
- To make adjectives from some countries we change the last letter to **ish** or **ese**. *Examples:* Ireland = Ir**ish**, China = Chin**ese**.
- To make adjectives from some countries we change the last letter to **an**. *Examples:* Mexico = Mexic**an**, Italy = Ital**ian**.
- To make adjectives from some countries we change the word altogether. *Example:* Holland = **Dutch**.

A Write the adjectives made from these countries. The adjectives end in **n**.

1 Jamaica   2 Australia   3 Canada
4 America   5 Uganda   6 Russia

B Write these sentences, making an adjective from the word in the brackets.

1 We like our _____ holidays. (Spain)
2 Mary was a _____ queen. (Scotland)
3 We eat _____ food with chopsticks. (China)
4 The _____ singer won the Eurovision Song Contest. (Sweden)

C Which country do each of these people come from?

1 Germans   2 Welsh   3 Belgians   4 Greeks
5 Pakistanis   6 French   7 Norwegians   8 Burmese

'ie' and 'ei' words

Many words contain **i** and **e** next to each other.
- Usually **i** comes first. *Examples:* f**ie**ld, ch**ie**f
- But sometimes **e** comes first. *Examples:* rec**ei**ve, c**ei**ling, h**ei**ght

There is a spelling rule which can help you:
'**i** before **e** except after **c**'.

Write down all the **ie** and **ei** words you can find hidden in this puzzle.

p	i	e	r	x	c	o	s
i	l	m	r	l	p	t	i
e	o	w	e	i	r	d	e
r	h	p	c	z	m	d	v
r	e	c	e	i	v	e	e
f	i	k	i	x	i	c	e
k	r	p	p	q	e	e	z
l	c	t	t	c	w	i	h
t	h	i	e	f	g	v	e
z	i	o	f	i	w	e	i
r	e	l	i	e	f	g	g
h	f	p	f	l	r	m	h
y	i	e	l	d	i	i	t

Watch out!
The **ie** spelling rule does not always work.
Examples:
h**ei**ght, w**ei**ght

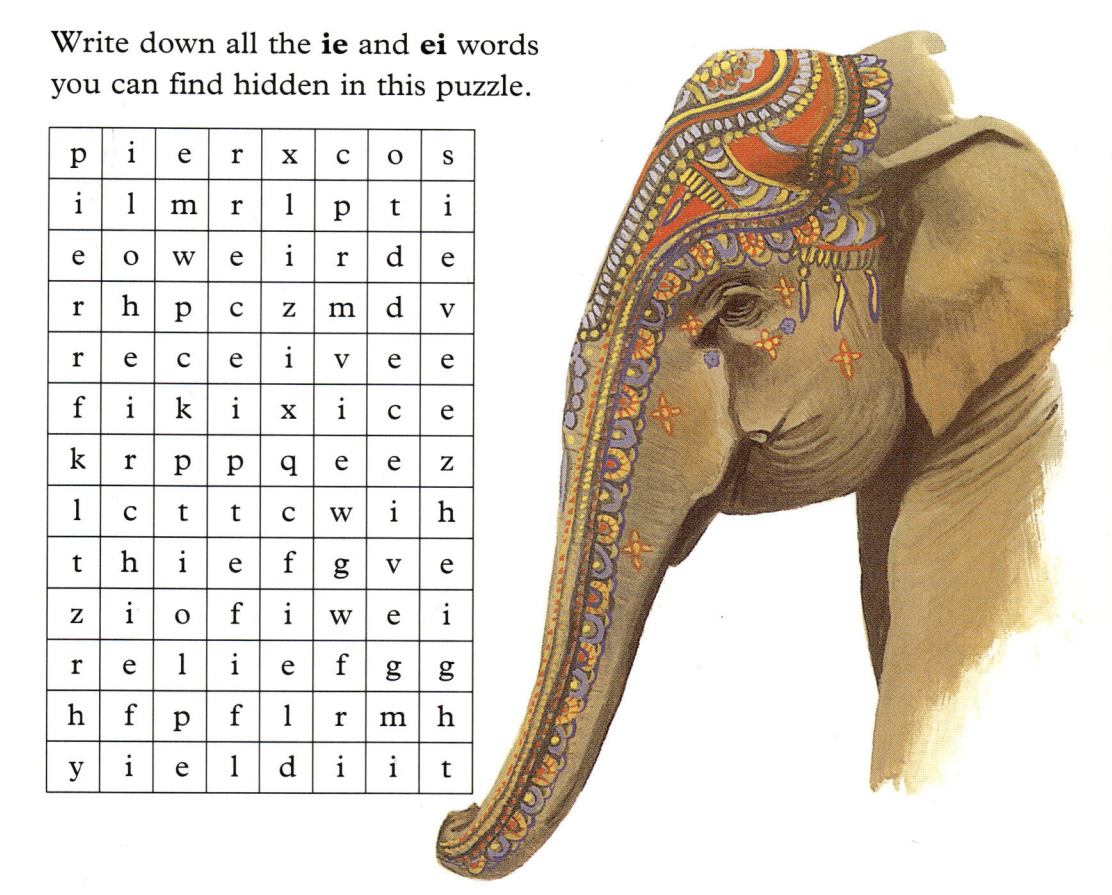

Be careful, one word appears twice.

WRITING SKILLS

Direct speech

Remember, **direct speech** is when you write the actual words a person has said.
Example: **"The Ganges is a wide river,"** said Sundip.
All the words inside the inverted commas are the words actually spoken.

A Write these sentences, putting inverted commas round the words actually spoken.

1 You must not enter the temple with shoes on, said Rajiv.
2 Father said, These waters have special powers.
3 My parents live in Delhi, said Reena.
4 Would you like to visit Varanasi? asked the guide.
5 Be careful, shouted the fisherman, or you'll damage my nets!

B Write a conversation between two friends who are wondering whether to go for an elephant ride. One person is trying to persuade the other, who is very nervous.

UNIT 9
Caves and underground rivers

Most of the largest caves in the world are formed in limestone. Limestone is a strong, tough rock, but it has one important weakness, it slowly dissolves in water. As water seeps through limestone it carries tiny amounts of the rock away. The dissolved limestone is carried in the water and deposited layer on layer to form spectacular shapes.

Water will eat its way into the limestone, dissolving some of the rock.

Some gaps between the rocks become so big they 'swallow' whole rivers. These cave entrances are called potholes.

Underground waterfall

Rubble on the floor is evidence of rock falling from the roof.

Many caves have magnificent shapes formed from limestone deposits dripping from the roof over thousands of years.

Stalactites

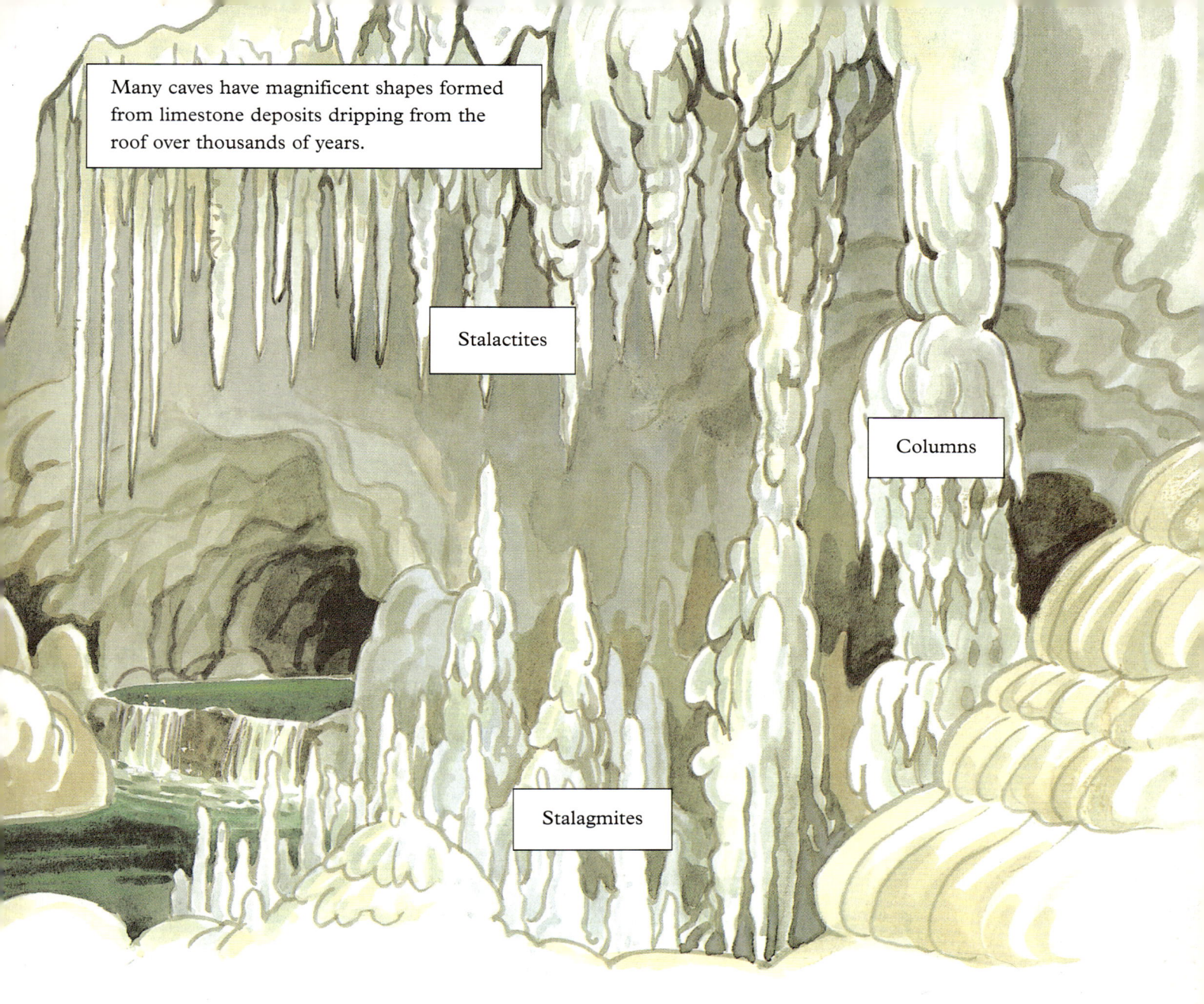

Columns

Stalagmites

COMPREHENSION SKILLS

A Copy these sentences. Fill in the missing words.
1 Caves are often found in _____ rocks.
2 Pointed shapes hanging from cave roofs are called _____ .
3 Pointed shapes on the floors of caves are called _____ .
4 Cave entrances are sometimes called _____ .

B Write sentences to answer each question.
1 Why are there so many caves in limestone rock?
2 How are stalactites formed?
3 What is a pothole?
4 Why do you think people want to explore caves?

LANGUAGE SKILLS

Superlatives

We know that when we want to compare more than two people or things we often add **es** to the adjective. This is called the **superlative** form of the adjective.
Examples: deep, deep**est**   large, larg**est**
If the adjective ends in **y** then we usually need to change the **y** to **i** before adding **est**.
Examples: sunny, sunn**iest**   dirty, dirt**iest**

Copy these adjectives and next to each write the superlative.

busy	heavy	mighty	noisy	
pretty	dusty	lively	furry	lovely

'ness' suffix

The **ness** suffix is a common ending, especially for **abstract nouns**. We cannot actually see or touch abstract nouns, but we can experience them.
Examples: sad, sad**ness**   ill, ill**ness**
There was complete dark**ness** in the cave.

A Make **ness** words from these root words, and put each one in a sentence.

1 weak   2 thoughtful   3 dry   4 kind

Look
Cover
Remember
Write
Check

Here is a useful rule to remember when adding **ness** to a word. If the word ends in **y** (and the **y** makes an 'ee' sound), change the **y** to an **i** and then add **ness**.
Examples: lazy, lazi**ness**   ugly, ugl**iness**

B Now make **ness** words from these root words.

1 happy   2 empty   3 heavy   4 nasty   5 busy

Root words

Root words are the simple words from which other words grow,
Examples: **work**   worker   working   worked
happy   happily   happiness   happier   unhappy

Make as many words as you can from these root words.

1 strong = strength, stronger, strongest, strongly

2 forget   3 dust   4 explore

WRITING SKILLS

Over-used words

Long ago 'nice' used to mean 'stupid' or 'silly'!

nice and **got** are two of the most over-used words in the English language. There is usually a better word to use.

A Write the first paragraph replacing the word **nice** with other words. The words in the box may help you. Sometimes it is better simply to leave out the word **nice**.

> sunny hot warm good smart flashy expensive best
> kind generous smart shining enjoyable short
> interesting impressive huge fun delicious

It was a **nice** day. It was **nice** to see the sun shining. I put on my **nice** new trainers. We were going with my **nice** uncle and aunty in their **nice** new car. They said it would be **nice** to take us for a **nice** trip to see the **nice** caves near where they live. We had a **nice** time and **nice** things to eat.

B Now write the next paragraph out, replacing the word **got** with other words. The words in the box may help you. Sometimes it is better simply to leave out the word **got**, or to change one or two of the other words as well.

> reached arrived climbed clambered jumped called
> fetched prepared bought must need to wrapped

When we **got** home we thanked them for the enjoyable day. We **got** out of the car and ran and **got** Mum to see Uncle and Aunty.
"We have **got** a meal for you to eat with us," said Mum.
"No thank you, we have **got** to go home. We have **got** a lot of work to do," replied our uncle.
"Just wait a minute then, for I've **got** a small present for you," said Mum.

45

UNIT 10
The days of the banyan tree

> **Autobiographies**
> The word **autobiography** comes from three Greek words:
> *auto* = self   *bios* = life   *graphos* = writing
> It is a story written by someone about his/her own life.

Here is a part of an autobiography by Madhur Jaffrey about her childhood in India.

There was an old banyan tree that grew just outside our house. It was more than a tree, it seemed to be a whole forest, all by itself.

Its trunk went up, up, and up, almost a hundred feet. Some of the branches, instead of rising and spreading like outstretched arms, made nosedives towards the earth, where they burrowed in, took root, and reappeared as fresh trunks. My nanny – or *aya*, as we called her – said that the roots of a banyan tree went all the way to the Underworld and that when they rose again as fresh trunks, they carried up with them all sorts of ghosts and goblins. She insisted that there never was a banyan tree without a few ghosts lurking in its branches.

I believed her.

My grandmother, on the other hand, said that the banyan tree was a blessed tree because it had the wisdom of its years and because it provided so much shade. In fact, in the burning months of May and June, we prayed to it and offered it the best of the summer's yield – seedless cucumbers, watermelons, aubergines and mangoes.

I saw my grandmother's point. In the summer, scorching winds blasted in from neighbouring deserts carrying with them particles of sand to irritate eyes and parch throats. When the sky overhead felt like an oven with its door left open by some careless cook, the banyan trees offered cool, natural arbours to perspiring travellers.

My grandmother always advised me, 'On your way back from school, remember to get off your bicycle and rest under the shade of the banyan tree.'

Rest under the banyan tree and bump into a ghost!

Oh dear me, no! I paid no attention to my grandmother. In fact, when I reached the banyan trees, I held my breath and bicycled for my life.

No ghosts were going to catch me!

Madhur Jaffrey

Glossary

nanny or *aya* is someone who is trained to look after children

COMPREHENSION SKILLS

Read the passage and answer the questions.

1 Why did the banyan tree seem to be 'a whole forest, all by itself'?
2 What is the Underworld?
3 Write the words and phrases that tell you how hot it was in the area where the banyan tree grew.
4 Why did the writer ignore her grandmother's advice?

LANGUAGE SKILLS

Prefix 'al'

'All right' is always two words.

> A **prefix** is added to the beginning of a word.
> 'All' means everyone or everything. But when words begin with this, the prefix **al** is spelt with only one 'l'.
> *Example:* **al**ways

Look at the words in the box.

almighty	almost	already	also
although	altogether	always	

Now write some sentences to include all of these words.

Suffix 'ful'

What is special about *beautiful*?

> A **suffix** is added to the end of a word.
> The suffix **ful** may be added to the end of some words to make an adjective ('describing' word). Notice that it also has only one 'l'.
> *Examples:* use, use**ful**   help, help**ful**

A Use the suffix **ful** to fill the gaps when you write these sentences. The word in brackets is a clue.

1. Her scratch was very _____. (pain)
2. His teacher said he'd been _____. (help)
3. My father is _____ that he will soon get a new job. (hope)
4. I find my dictionary very _____. (use)
5. My new baby sister is _____. (beauty)
6. Be _____ when you cross the road in busy traffic. (care)
7. I couldn't sleep and was _____ all night. (wake)
8. Some people become more _____ as they get older. (forget)
9. The young animals were very _____. (play)
10. It is _____ the way he treats his animals. (shame)

B Make up three sentences of your own to use these **ful** words.

wonderful   hurtful   spiteful

WRITING SKILLS

Writing about yourself

When you keep a diary you are writing a sort of autobiography. You can look back on it when you are older and it will remind you of the things you did, the people you knew and how you felt about things that happened to you.

Autobiographies usually tell the reader about:

- where and when the writer was born
- the major events in the writer's life
- the people who were important in the writer's life

You can begin to think about this sort of information by drawing a time line.

Deepak's time line:

| born
March 1984 | brother's birth
May 1988 | moved house
July 1989 | began school
Sept. 1989 | met Dan my
best friend 1990 |

1 Draw a time line for the important events in your life.

Sometimes there is one particular thing that you remember very clearly from your childhood.
Madhur Jaffrey remembered the banyan tree.
When she wrote about the banyan tree she:

- described the tree in detail because her readers may never have seen a banyan tree
- told us about what her grandmother said and what her aya said
- made it clear why she remembered the banyan tree – because it frightened her.

2 Write about something that happened when you were younger. It might have been a special treat, something you enjoyed very much or something that frightened you.
You must remember that your reader was not there at the time so:

- describe what happened clearly
- explain about the people who were involved
- make it clear why you remember this particular thing by showing how you felt about it.

49

Writing letters

Some letters are a kind of autobiography.

When you write a letter to friends you usually tell them about what you have been doing and if anything special or awful has happened.

Imagine you have a penfriend in America called Mary Ann who has never visited you. Your penfriend sent you a letter and a birthday card, and wants to know how you celebrated your birthday.

Now you are going to write back because it is her birthday. Here are some things to think about before you begin to write.

Remember how to set out a letter.

- **How you will begin your letter:**
  – remember it is Mary Ann's birthday.
  – she has sent you a letter and a birthday card for *your* birthday.
- **Writing about your birthday:**
  – how old are you?
  – did you have a party?
  – did you go out for a treat?
  – did your friends celebrate your birthday with you?
  – did everything go well?
  – did something go wrong?
  – what presents were you given?
- **How you will end the letter:**
  – do you want to know how Mary Ann will celebrate her birthday?
  – do you want to know anything else about life in America?

Personal details

When you go to a new doctor, fill in a form, or many other things. you will be asked questions about yourself.

These questions are to find out about your **personal details** – that is, things about **you**.

1 Copy the chart into your book and fill it in.

   You may have to ask for help at home.

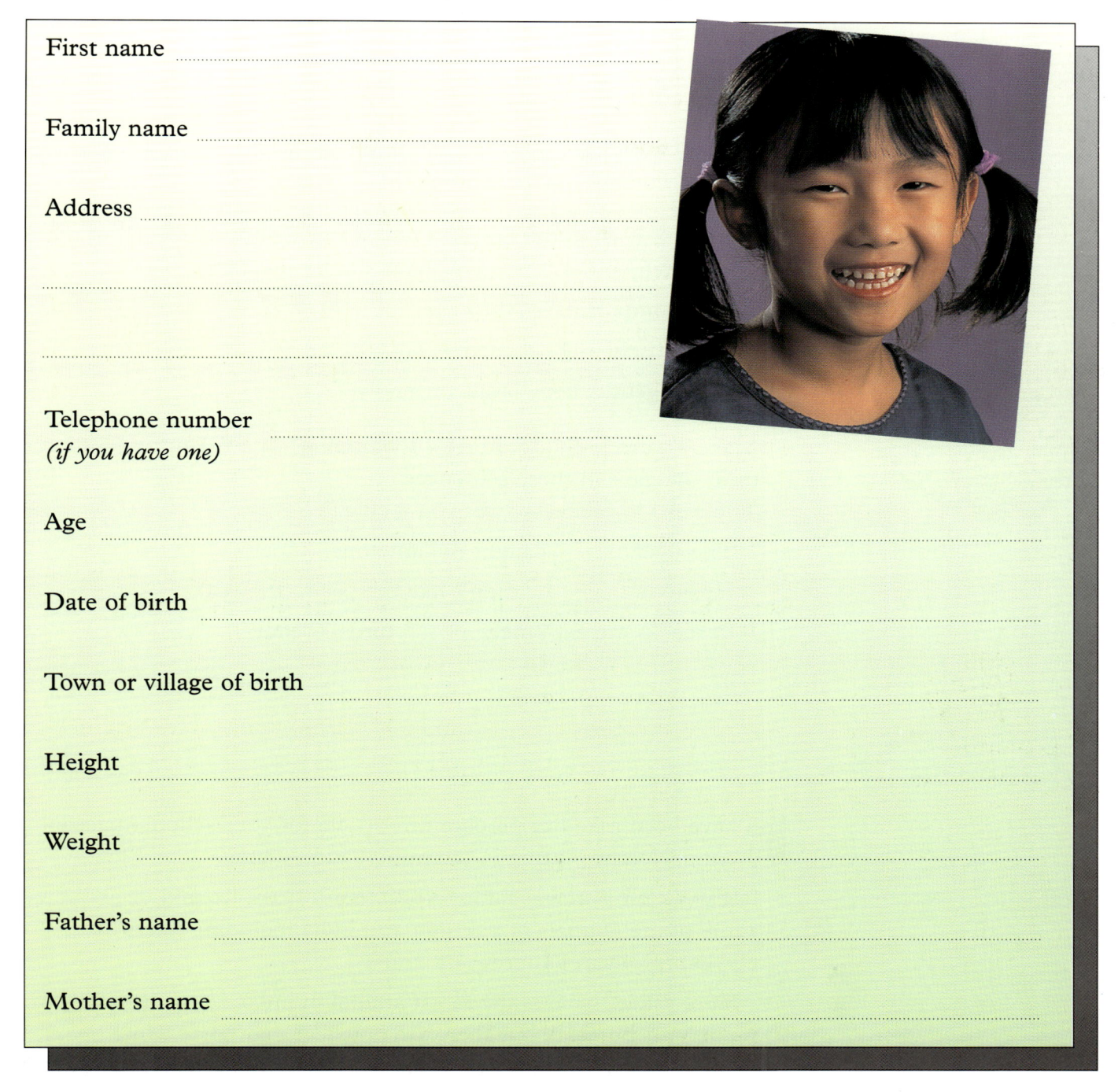

First name	
Family name	
Address	
Telephone number (if you have one)	
Age	
Date of birth	
Town or village of birth	
Height	
Weight	
Father's name	
Mother's name	

2 Can you think of any other **personal details** to add to your chart?

Check-up 2

VOCABULARY

A Make adjectives from countries to describe these creatures.
1 _____ elephant (India)   2 _____ elephant (Africa)
3 _____ geese (Canada)   4 _____ cattle (Wales)
5 _____ horses (Spain)   6 _____ goats (France)

B Write the odd-one-out in these groups.
Give a reason for each answer.
1 dog, cat, horse, eagle, goat
2 lion, kangaroo, tiger, cheetah, leopard
3 man, woman, mouse, boy, girl

C Choose a word in the brackets which is a synonym of each of these words. Remember, synonyms have similar meanings.
1 leap (jump, run, fly, fall)
2 pretty (ugly, rich, attractive, noisy)
3 fierce (gentle, lion, savage, friendly)

D Make a word with an **al** prefix (beginning) or a **ful** suffix (ending) to fit the gaps in these sentences.
The word in brackets gives you a clue.
1 The tiger _____ caught the antelope. (most)
2 He ate it _____ he didn't like the taste. (though)
3 Peacocks are extremely _____ birds. (beauty)

PUNCTUATION

You have been asked to prepare this article for your school magazine. Write it correctly, putting in the punctuation marks.

last week mr purewal came to talk to our class. he told us about some of the animals in pakistan and india including tigers elephants vultures cobras and kraits

laura asked, what is the rarest animal in india. i cant be sure replied mr purewal, but there are now less than forty white tigers

we all enjoyed his really interesting talk and our teacher mrs varma thanked him and asked him to come again soon. he said he would

GRAMMAR

A Find conjunctions to join these pairs of sentences, to make them more interesting to read. Write the new sentences in full.
1 The wolf's jaw is powerful. It can pick up an egg without cracking it.
2 The lioness had two cubs this year. She only had one cub last year.
3 The bee-keeper wears protective clothing. He doesn't want to be stung.
4 The seal searched and searched along the beach. She found her lost pup.

B Write the past tense of each of these verbs.
1 run = ran   2 jump   3 bite   4 find
5 say   6 fall   7 throw   8 come
9 swim   10 walk   11 dance   12 steal

C Copy each sentence, putting an apostrophe (') in the right place.
1 Janes kitten meowed.   2 The two kittens mother is black.
3 A lions head appeared.   4 Look at Delroys hamster.
5 Surinders pony was grazing.   6 The bears cage was cleaned.

SPELLING

A Write these words, filling in the missing letters with **ie** or **ei**.
1 f_ld   2 rec_ve   3 ch_f   4 p_ce
5 c_ling   6 th_f   7 w_rd   8 p_r

B Write the plurals of these words.
1 cockatoo   2 bamboo   3 piano   4 motto
5 volcano   6 cello   7 potato   8 tomato
9 echo   10 photo   11 solo   12 radio

C Write these words, filling in the missing letters with **c** or **s**.
1 mi_e   2 fa_e   3 ra_e   4 sin_e
5 co_y   6 chan_e   7 pala_e   8 ri_e
9 dan_e   10 noi_e   11 fier_e   12 hor_e

UNIT 11
Forests

The Lord of the Rings

Read about Frodo's journey through the old forest.

They picked a way among the trees, and their ponies plodded along, carefully avoiding the many writhing and interlacing roots. There was no undergrowth. The ground was rising steadily, and as they went forward it seemed that the trees became taller, darker, and thicker. There was no sound, except an occasional drip of moisture falling through the still leaves. For the moment there was no whispering or movement among the branches; but they all got an uncomfortable feeling that they were being watched with disapproval … The feeling steadily grew, until they found themselves looking up quickly, or glancing back over their shoulders, as if they expected a sudden blow …

Frodo began to wonder if it were possible to find a way through, and if he had been right to make the others come into this abominable wood.

J R R Tolkien

Glossary
writhing means twisting about
interlacing means tangled

COMPREHENSION SKILLS

A Read the passage and answer the questions.

1 Write the words and phrases that the writer uses to describe the forest.

2 How does the description of the forest make you feel?

3 Do you think Frodo and his friends enjoy the ride through the forest?

4 Why does the writer call it an 'abominable wood'?

5 Find the words in the passage that mean the same as:
 – keeping away from
 – happening now and then
 – speaking in a soft, low voice.

Learning about forests

Look at the diagram and notes on the forest.

1 The top layer of the forest is called the **canopy**. The leaves of the tallest trees push their way into the sunlight. They need the energy from the sun to grow.

2 Underneath the canopy the forest is dark. The sun is blotted out by the leaves of the tall trees. Here you can see the trunks of the largest trees, smaller trees and bushes.

3 The **shrub layer** is on the floor of the forest. Here plants and herbs grow and animals that live on the floor of the forest can be seen.

4 Underneath the plants and herbs you will find mosses and a lot of insect life. This layer is called the **ground layer**.

B 1 What is the top layer of the forest called?

2 Why is the sun important for trees?

3 What is it like underneath the canopy?

4 What would you find on the floor of the forest?

5 Where would you find mosses and insect life?

6 Can you tell if the writer likes or dislikes the forest?

LANGUAGE SKILLS

Prefixes

> Letters added at the front of a word to change the meaning are called a **prefix**. **Dis**, **un**, **in** or **im** prefixes can change the word to its antonym (or opposite meaning).
>
> *Example:* Frodo and his friends think that someone or something is watching them with **dis**approval.
>
> approval = like   **dis**approval = do not like

A These words make their opposites by using the prefix **dis**.
Write the meaning of each word and its antonym (opposite).
Use a dictionary if you need help.

1 agree   2 trust   3 embark   4 like   5 obey

B Choose a prefix **un**, **in** or **im** to make the antonyms of these words.

1 happy   2 perfect   3 cover   4 possible   5 capable

C Put any three of your antonyms in sentences to show their meanings.

WRITING SKILLS

What type of writing is it?

When you are going to write something you need to think about why you are writing it. These questions will help.

- Is it an imaginative piece of writing?
  Some of what you write about may be true but you can make things up, invent characters and write about strange things that could never really happen, for example:

  stories
  poems
  descriptions of imaginary places and people
  plays.

- Is it a factual piece of writing?
  You may need to find out about something by using reference books, for example:

  writing about historical events
  reports of scientific experiments
  notes, charts, diagrams for geography, history, etc.

- Are you writing about something that really happened, either to yourself or someone else? This could be:

  diaries
  autobiography
  letters.

Who is my audience?

- Myself – personal writing, for instance:

  diaries, notes.

- Other people – writing which other people will read, such as:

  travel brochures
  newspaper articles
  reports
  speeches
  stories
  descriptions

1 Now look at the two pieces of writing about the forest. Answer these questions for each piece of writing.

   a What type of writing is it?

   b Who was the writer writing for?

2 Look at the types of writing in the box below.
  Make three headings in your book:

Writing for myself   Writing for people I know   Writing for people I don't know

Think about each type of writing and put it in the right list. Some may go in more than one list.

letters	menus	instructions	stories
shopping lists		speeches	newspaper articles
adverts	poems	diaries	reports
telephone messages		notes	plays	maps

UNIT 12
Bushfire

Five children are caught up in a bushfire that sweeps across dry grassland in the outback of Australia. They are searching for a friend called Shane. Jan set out alone, and is separated from the others. Suddenly they find that they are trapped and in danger of being caught by the fire.

They plunged on. Sometimes they were engulfed in clouds of smoke like stinking yellow mountain mist, but Bill knew the way so well that he went forward unerringly.

Suddenly he stopped. 'Listen! A coo-ee!'

The long-drawn out first syllable floated to them on the smoke, followed by the whip-like ending.

'Jan?'

Jan was coo-eeing. It did not sound very loud; there were too many other noises to drown the call.

They listened. Each coo-ee came nearer. It was unlikely that she thought they would be on this track; probably she wanted anyone at all who might be in this vicinity to know she was there.

'She's coming back – coming this way!'

Then Jan came out of the smoke. She was crying, and so distraught that she didn't ask how or why they were there. Perhaps she understood. Shane was their friend, too.

'Fire's right across the track! We can't get through!'

'How near?'

'Quarter of a mile, p'raps. Not burning as fast now. But creeping up over everything, swallowing everything …

'I can't get through. I can't get through to Shane!' Jan was streaked with grime and smoke and tears …

Now they realised that the wind was not altogether subdued by the cold front. That a fierce gust had arisen again, and fire was spotting over their heads. Fire-brands were lobbing behind them. A series of missiles, as though the fire had suddenly found its mark, and was aiming with accuracy. It would veer again but not before its mischief had been done. It had all the viciousness of fire out of control … of wildfire.

Bill knew, and the others were scarcely less quick to realise, that retreat was cut off.

from 'Wildfire' by *Mavis Thorpe Clark*

Glossary

engulfed means swallowed up
vicinity means nearby
distraught means upset
p'raps means perhaps

subdued means calmed
fire-brands are burning pieces of wood
retreat is the way back

COMPREHENSION SKILLS

True or false?

1 Bill was unsure of the way to go.
2 Jan's call was not very loud.
3 She was calling because she knew that her friends were on the track.
4 The wind was blowing the fire towards them.
5 The only way to safety was to go back.

LANGUAGE SKILLS

Choosing words

The painting shows a bushfire in Africa.
You could describe this quite simply by saying:

    Hunters and animals are caught in a big fire.

This is what the picture is about but the sentence does not tell you very much.

To describe the picture properly you need to think about the words you can use to describe what you can see and also what you think the animals and the hunters are feeling.

Look at the fire.

1. Make a list of words that describe its colour and size.
   - How is the fire burning?
   - Is it gentle?
   - Is it raging out of control?

Look at the animals.

2. Make a list of words to describe how they are moving.
   - Are they strolling about?
   - Are they leaping wildly?

Look at the hunters.

3. Make a list of words to describe how you think they are feeling.
   - Are they calm and untroubled?
   - Are they panicking and alarmed?

'fire' words

Put each of these **fire** words into a sentence.
Use a dictionary to help you.

fire-alarm

fire-fighter

fire-brand

fire-brigade

fire-escape

fire-eater

WRITING SKILLS

Story endings

Read the passage on pages 60-61 again and think how you might end the story. The kind of ending you write will depend on how you want your reader to feel.

1 **Happy ever after**

The children quickly find a way out of the fire.
A storm blows up and the rain puts the fire out.
No one is hurt.

2 **Fear and excitement**

The children find it very difficult to escape. They try one way and then another and they are always cut off by the fire. Just when there seems to be no hope, they are rescued and taken to safety.

3 Sadness The children eventually escape from the fire but one of them is hurt badly on the way.

4 Unexpectedly surprised The children are trapped and there is no way out. A spacecraft lands from another planet and rescues them.

Each of these endings will make the reader feel different. **Choose one of these ideas, or write your own ending** to the story but make sure you know how you want your readers to feel when they have finished.

UNIT 13
Fascinating body facts

More than half an adult person is water! For a man that's about 40 litres – enough to fill four pairs of large boots.

Each red blood cell travels round the body 172,000 times before it dies after about four months.

The fastest human muscle can make our eyelids blink at about five times a second.

If you could lay all your veins and arteries out they would stretch 22 times round the world!

Our hearts beat at about 70 times a minute. An elephant's heart beats at 25 times each minute and a mouse's heart at 600 times a minute.

The record for the longest hair is held by Madras, a monk, whose hair was 8·8 metres when he died in 1949.

Most of us have about 100,000 hairs on our scalp.

On very hot days we lose up to two litres of sweat.

The nails on the right hand of a right-handed person grow faster than nails on the left hand, and vice versa.

Your hand and wrist contain 27 bones.

The tallest person ever was Robert Wadlow, at 2 metres 72 centimetres tall. The shortest adult ever was Pauline Musters, at 59 centimetres.

The most babies ever born to one mother was 69. Mrs Vassilyev had 16 pairs of twins, 7 sets of triplets and 4 sets of quads.

COMPREHENSION SKILLS

A Copy these sentences. Fill in the missing words or numbers.

1 The human heart beats at about _____ times a minute.

2 _____ holds the record for the longest hair.

3 The shortest adult person ever was _____ .

4 A mouse's heart beats _____ than an elephant's.

B Write a sentence to answer each question.

1 Does an elephant's heart beat faster or slower than a human's?

2 On which of your hands do the nails grow faster?

3 Would you have liked to have been one of Mrs Vassilyev's children? Why?

4 Would you have preferred to be Pauline Musters or Robert Wadlow? What are the main reasons for your choice?

LANGUAGE SKILLS

Irregular adjective forms

Remember, when we make the comparative form of an adjective we add **er**, **ier** or **more**; and when we make the superlative form of the adjective we add **est**, **iest** or **most**.

However, a few adjectives do not follow these rules. They change completely in their comparative and superlative forms. We simply need to learn them. Don't worry, there aren't many!

adjective	comparative	superlative
bad	worse	worst
good	better	best
little	less	least
much	more	most
many	more	most

A Copy these sentences, choosing one word from the box below to fill each gap.

> worse   good   many   best   less   bad
> more   little   better   least   much   worst   most

1 Mrs Vassilyev had the _____ babies ever born to one woman.
2 Dad is nearly bald, so he has _____ hair than me, and he has the _____ amount of hair in our family.
3 Our baby has a _____ cough. It is _____ than mine.
4 The male duck is _____ colourful than the female.

B Copy this table, filling in the missing words.

adjective	comparative	superlative
small	smaller	smallest
big	bigger	____
____	prettier	____
funny	____	____
____	____	most beautiful
fat	____	____
terrible	____	____
____	more frightening	____
____	worse	____
little	____	____

'ible' and 'able' endings

Here are some important words which have **ible** endings, which are sometimes confused with **able** endings:

horr**ible**   terr**ible**   poss**ible**   sens**ible**   respons**ible**
vis**ible**   forc**ible**   incred**ible**   ed**ible**   leg**ible**

A Write three sentences which include as many **ible** words as possible.

B Make a list of words which have **able** endings.

Auxiliary verbs

Auxiliary verbs are sometimes called 'helper' verbs.

Sometimes we need more than one verb to make a sentence work properly. We need to use auxiliary verbs to help the main verb.
Examples: He **has** visited the moon. He **is** visiting the moon.
He **will** visit the moon.

A Copy these sentences, filling in the gaps with one of these auxiliary verbs.

| have | can | should | could | has |

1 I _____ visited my dentist for a check-up.
2 Doctors _____ perform very clever operations.
3 We _____ offer our seats to old people on buses.
4 You _____ hurt yourself if you fall over.
5 He _____ run all the way home.

B Copy three sentences from a reading book and underline the main verbs in red and any auxiliary verbs in blue.

WRITING SKILLS

Short story

Write a short story with a beginning, a middle and an end, using as many of these **age** words as you can.
You are not allowed to use more than eight sentences, so you will need to think carefully about each one.

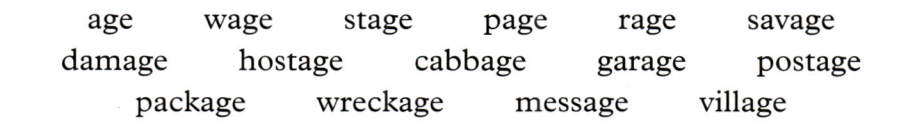

age	wage	stage	page	rage	savage
damage	hostage	cabbage	garage	postage
package	wreckage	message	village

UNIT 14
Printing and writing

When we write we use a pen or a pencil. We make marks that communicate meaning to the person that reads it.

When we print something we can do it over and over again without having to write it out every time.

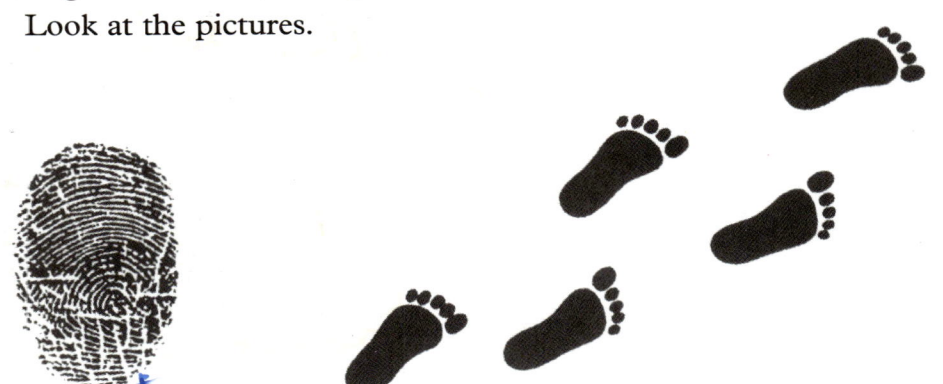

Look at the pictures.

Printing words works in the same way as making fingerprints or footprints.

The first form of printing was with wooden blocks. Parts of the wood were cut away leaving the words or pictures raised. They were covered with ink and pressed onto paper.

This was how printing began.

Cutting these blocks of wood was a slow process. Around the middle of the fifteenth century three men called Gutenberg, Fust and Schöffer made single letters out of metal. They arranged the letters to make the words they wanted for one page, and then they could rearrange them for the next page and so on. This was known as moveable type and was a great step forward in printing.

Printing Office 1619

Two people who are famous because of the work they did with printing are Johannes Gutenberg and William Caxton.

Look at the fact file for Johannes Gutenberg.

Name:	Johannes Gutenberg
Born:	around 1400
Died:	around 1468
Nationality:	German
What he is famous for:	Invented a method of printing with moveable type. 1445 produced the printed Gutenberg Bible.

COMPREHENSION SKILLS

A Read the passage and answer the questions.

1 What is the main difference between printing and writing?

2 Make a list of some things which have printed words.

3 Make a list of things which have the same picture/design printed over and over again.

4 What is the purpose of the piece of writing about printing and writing?

5 Which audience is it written for?

B Do some research on William Caxton by using reference books and encyclopedias.

With the information you find make a fact file on William Caxton.

LANGUAGE SKILLS

Present and past tense

> When we write about something which is happening now, we are using the **present tense**.
> When we write about something which happened in the past, we change the verb. This usually means adding a **d** or **ed** to the end as a suffix. We are then using the **past tense**. Most newspaper reports are written in the past tense.
>
> *present tense*   *past tense*
> *Example:* We **live** now.   Our ancestors **lived** long ago.

A Write these sentences as if they happened in the past. Change the verbs to the past tense.

1 I walk to school.
2 Gill delivers the papers.
3 We play football.
4 We are celebrating the festival.

B Copy this table. Fill in the missing words.

verb	present tense	past tense
hop	hopping	____
jump	____	jumped
help	helping	____
clean	cleaning	____
sail	sailing	____
paint	____	painted

WRITING SKILLS

Interviews

You had to rely on what other people had written about William Caxton to write your fact file.

If the person who is being written about is still alive then he/she can be interviewed. This means that someone will talk to them and write about what they say.

Choose someone in your class to interview. Just as with story writing you need to plan what you are going to do:

What kind of information do you need?

Make a list of six questions that you will ask the person you are going to write about, such as:

- Where and when were you born?
- Have you moved house, school?
- What are your hobbies?

You can think of a lot more.

Interviewing and taking notes

Ask the questions and make notes about what the person says. Remember you do not have to write down every word at this stage. These notes are only for you to use later.

Writing up the interview

Write up the interview in two ways:

1 **As a playscript:**
   Sally: When were you born?
   Javinder: In 1985.
   Sally: Have you always lived in Nairobi?
   Javinder: No, we moved from Delhi when I was three.

2 **As a piece of factual writing:**
   Javinder was born in 1985. He lived in Delhi until he was three and then moved to Nairobi.

Checking your information

When you have written up your notes, go back to the person you have interviewed and let him/her read it. You can make any changes they want and then write out the final draft.

UNIT 15
Earth

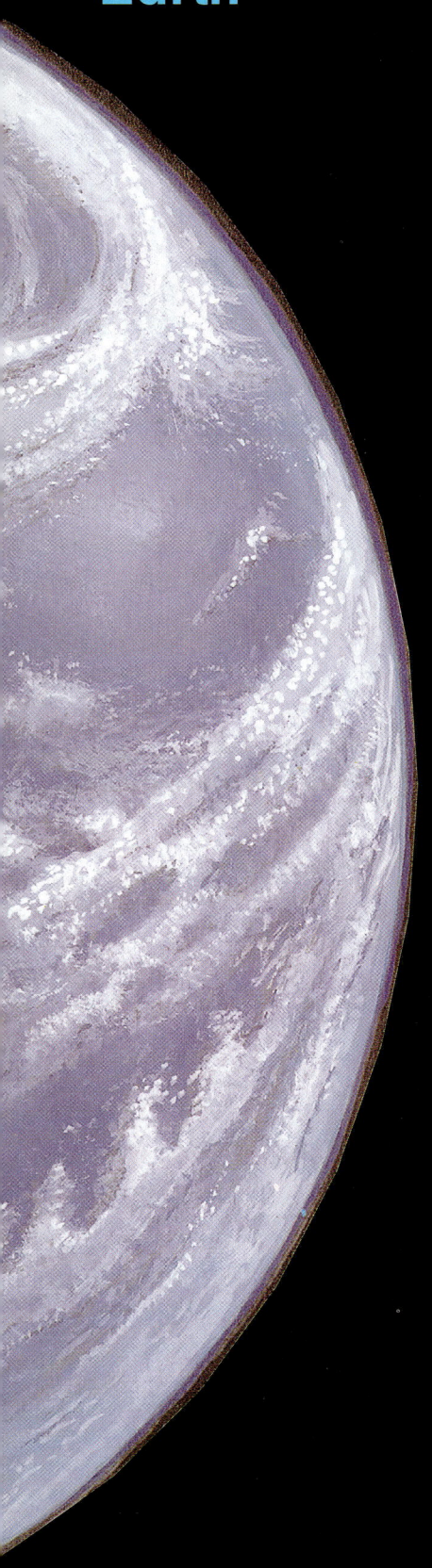

I am your favourite planet,
The one that gave you birth,
A green spot,
A clean spot,
That's known as Mother Earth.

My orbit never changes
On my journey round the Sun,
Circling through Space,
Leaving no trace.
(Each lap means one year gone.)

I spin upon my axis
Once every day and night;
Observers say
I lean one way;
I'm inclined to think they're right!

I have a Moon that sometimes comes
Between the Sun and me;
And for a time
I know that I'm
Plunged in obscurity.

Consider the Sun, Moon and Stars,
The other eight planets and I.
Ask, "Who put them in place?
Who arranged them in Space?
When did it happen and why?"

Experts say the whole Scheme will collapse
And there's nothing that mankind can do.
Not much longer to go –
A billion light years or so –
So I'm not going to worry. Are you?

Charles Connell

COMPREHENSION SKILLS

A Copy these sentences. Fill in the missing words.
1 Earth orbits around the _____ .
2 Each orbit of the Sun takes _____ year.
3 There are _____ planets apart from the Earth.
4 The poet says Earth will last for a _____ years.

B Write sentences to answer each question.
1 How long does it take Earth to spin once on its axis?
2 What sometimes comes between Earth and the Sun?
3 Where does the Earth's orbit take it?
4 Why is the poet not going to worry about the collapse of the universe?

LANGUAGE SKILLS

Gender words

Sometimes some things, like 'ships', are given masculine or feminine names; but they are really neuter.

Some words are **masculine** and some are **feminine**.
  Examples:
  sister = feminine (or female)   brother = masculine (or male)
Nouns can also be **common** or **neuter**.
  Examples:
  parent = common (because it can be feminine or masculine)
  planet = neuter (because it is neither feminine nor masculine)

A Copy these headings and write each of the words in the box under one of them.

feminine   masculine   common   neuter

space	father	Earth	Sun	parents	mother
her	him	teacher	they	you	princess	singer
cow	bull	calf	cowshed	field	policeman	he

B Find five words which change from masculine to feminine if **ess** or **ss** is added as a suffix. (Hint: you have just used one.)

C Write the masculine form of these words.

| grandmother | queen | aunt | hen |
| her | she | woman | nun | cow |

75

Syllables

> A **syllable** is a part of a word which can be said by itself. Each syllable has its own vowel sound.
> *Examples:* 'Planet' is pronounced **plan-et**, so it has two syllables.
> 'Village' is pronounce **vill-age**, so it also has two syllables.

A Copy the words in the box. Draw a line for each word to show the syllables. The first is done to help you.

1 village = vill/age

village   orbit   something   shining   ocean   often   picture

B Look at the poem at the beginning of this unit.

1 Find five words that have one syllable. (Like this: Earth)

2 Find five words that have two syllables (Like this: jour/ney)

3 Find as many words as you can that have three or more syllables. (Like this: ob/scur/it/y)

Adverbs

> Remember, adverbs tell us *how*, *when* or *where* the action of a verb takes place.
> *Examples:*
> The spaceship landed **awkwardly**. (*how*)
> The escape hatch opened **immediately**. (*when*)
> Firefighters rushed from **everywhere**. (*where*)

A Copy these sentences. Underline the adverbs.

1 They slowly lifted the injured people out.

2 The relatives looked on anxiously.

3 "Call an ambulance now!" shouted the doctor.

4 It arrived quickly.

5 "Bring a stretcher here," he called.

6 Happily, no one was killed in the accident.

B Find a different adverb to finish each of these sentences.

1 The girl ran _____ .   2 The girl sang _____ .

3 The girl danced _____ .   4 The girl shouted _____ .

5 The girl fell _____ .   6 The girl whispered _____ .

WRITING SKILLS

Science fiction

You have always wanted the new telescope that you have just been given for your birthday. But this one is even bigger and more powerful than you have ever dreamed you'd own! As soon as it gets dark, you carry it carefully outside and start to scan the sky. The stars and planets that have mystified and excited you since you were a small child look even more beautiful and colourful than you had imagined possible. You sweep the sky in stunned amazement until suddenly you see something which makes your heart miss a beat. In that instant you realise that what you always thought was a vast emptiness isn't empty at all …

Use a planning sheet to plan a story based on this beginning. Before you start writing, think carefully about the **plot**, the **characters** who will be in your story, and the **setting** of where the action will take place.

Make it the most exciting story you've ever written!

Check-up 3

VOCABULARY

A Copy this table and fill in the missing words.

adjective	comparative	superlative
big	bigger	biggest
small	___	___
busy	___	___
good	___	___
many	___	___
bad	___	___
happy	___	___
miserable	___	___
beautiful	___	___
interesting	___	___

B Write an antonym and a synonym for each of these words.

1 big = small (antonym);   large (synonym)

2 fast   3 tiny   4 happy   5 fracture   6 inside

C Copy this list of nouns. Next to each one write whether its gender is masculine, feminine, common or neuter.

1 aunt = feminine

2 father   3 hen   4 person

5 cabbage   6 princess   7 Moon

8 children   9 grandfather   10 cattle

D Write two sentences for each pair of homophones to show their differences in meaning. Use a dictionary to help you.

1 new/knew 2 threw/through 3 their/there 4 sure/shore

E Copy these sentences, filling in the gaps. The words in brackets will help you.

1 His teacher was cross when he _____ the school rules. (obeyed)
2 She was _____ because she had torn her best dress. (happy)
3 Ali tried, but it was _____ to balance one ball on top of another. (possible)
4 I _____ anyone being cruel to animals. (like)
5 They _____ the man who had cheated them once before. (trusted)

PUNCTUATION

A Read these sentences carefully. They each need editing because most of the punctuation and the capital letters are missing, and something is wrong with the words which are underlined.

1 joseph and louisa ran home to <u>sea</u> <u>there</u> uncle francis
2 bill delroy winston and faith were already <u>their</u>
3 it is certainly good to see you kids said uncle francis
4 <u>you're</u> cousins kendra joy and errol send you <u>there</u> love he said
5 shall i show you how to throw a frisbee asked their uncle
6 yes please shouted the children
7 oh dear me exclaimed Gran do be careful
8 crash went the glass in the window

B Use a pencil and ruler to draw the shape of an envelope. On the envelope write the name and address of a friend or relation.

GRAMMAR

A Copy these words and phrases and next to each one write whether it is about the present, past or future.

1 yesterday = past
2 today
3 now
4 next year
5 tomorrow
6 a fortnight ago
7 the day before yesterday
8 last century
9 in the year 2005
10 this minute
11 my next birthday
12 when I was a baby

B Write these sentences in the past tense.
1. I am eating my meal.
2. They are feeling hungry.
3. The animal creeps through the reeds towards the big bird.
4. I hate going to the dentist.

C Write sentences beginning with these words. Underline all the verbs you use. Don't forget the small auxiliary verbs.
1. At this moment …
2. Soon …
3. Last night …
4. During the last holiday …
5. After school tomorrow …
6. Next year …

D Copy these sentences and underline the adverbs.
1. He walked quickly.
2. She spoke truthfully.
3. Ali arrived at school early.
4. Roxanna came home today.
5. Darren played outside.
6. Ann went away.

E Think of adverbs which tell how these actions are done.
1. I ran _____.
2. It climbed _____.
3. She shouted _____.
4. They whispered _____.
5. She smiled _____.
6. He struggled _____.
7. She fell _____.
8. It moved _____.

SPELLING

A Write the words that are missing from these sentences.
1. Every sentence should begin with a ca_____ letter.
2. You have drawn a good pi_____.
3. She keeps her car in a ga_____ at night.
4. We went to the st_____ to get on the train.
5. He went into hospital and had an op_____ on his throat.